Quick
Change

Refresh a Room *Fast* with Quilted Bed Runners

Compiled by Karen M. Burns

Martingale
Create with Confidence

Quick Change: Refresh a Room Fast with
Quilted Bed Runners
© 2015 by Martingale & Company®

Martingale
19021 120th Ave. NE, Ste. 102
Bothell, WA 98011-9511 USA
ShopMartingale.com

Printed in China
20 19 18 17 16 15   8 7 6 5 4 3 2 1

Library of Congress Cataloging-in-Publication Data
is available upon request.

ISBN: 978-1-60468-583-1

MISSION STATEMENT

Dedicated to providing quality products and service
to inspire creativity.

CREDITS

PUBLISHER AND CHIEF VISIONARY OFFICER
Jennifer Erbe Keltner

EDITORIAL DIRECTOR
Karen Costello Soltys

DESIGN DIRECTOR
Paula Schlosser

ACQUISITIONS EDITOR
Karen M. Burns

PHOTOGRAPHER
Brent Kane

TECHNICAL EDITOR
Rebecca Kemp Brent

PRODUCTION MANAGER
Regina Girard

COPY EDITOR
Tiffany Mottet

COVER AND
INTERIOR DESIGNER
Adrienne Smitke

ILLUSTRATOR
Anne Moscicki

SPECIAL THANKS

Martingale thanks Elke and Don Spivey of
Clearview, WA, and David Owen Hastings
of Lynnwood, WA, for generously allowing
the photography for this book to take
place in their homes.

CONTENTS

Introduction

What does the master bedroom of your dreams look like? Is it a crisp cottage-style bungalow? A zen-like retreat? A colorful inspiration zone? A timeless classic suite? Or maybe it's a beachy getaway? And how about your guest room? Do you long to create a fresh and inviting space to welcome overnight visitors, but worry that one style won't suit all?

Dreaming of all the possibilities is fun, but making those dreams a reality is even better. That's where the idea for *Quick Change* was born. What if you could change the entire look and feel of a bedroom by swapping out only a bed runner and a few accessories? Fabulous!

We enlisted the imaginations of several best-selling designers to turn this idea into a how-to book of bed runner patterns. But beyond that, we've tried to show you in the accompanying photos how just a few small changes to your accessories and a few pillow or pillowcase swaps can change the look of a room entirely. It's an economical way to freshen your decor without undertaking a total makeover.

An added bonus: storing alternate bed runners takes a lot less space than storing extra bed-sized quilts.

To convey our ideas, you'll find the book divided into four groupings, each with a solid throw or coverlet that coordinates with the combination of runners in that section. We sorted groupings by color palettes—"Ocean Blues," "Summertime," "Rich and Earthy," and "Bold and Bright"— but since any of the runners can be made in colors to suit your style, you should feel free to select the ones you love best for your "Quick Change" setting. And while you're at it, imagine that a bed runner doesn't always have to go across the foot of the bed. If you prefer to run it top to bottom, go for it! We think it adds a little personality to the look and draws more attention to your fabric creation.

Whatever your style, know that you can complete any of these stylish runners in a fraction of the time it would take to complete a bed-sized quilt. Which means more time to make more runners. And that translates into more looks you'll love. Enjoy!

Ocean Blues

Winding Roads

Striking value changes combine with simply pieced Log Cabin blocks in this bed runner. The result is an easy project with surprisingly complex design.

By Megan Jimenez of Quilt Story

FINISHED SIZE: 25" x 102"

Materials

Yardage is based on 42"-wide fabric. Fat quarters are approximately 18" x 21". The bed runner shown was made using Color Me Happy by V and Co. for Moda Fabrics.

1 fat quarter *each* of 7 light prints for blocks

1 fat quarter *each* of 13 dark-green or dark-blue prints for blocks

⅝ yard of green print for binding

3 yards of fabric for backing

31" x 108" piece of batting

Cutting

From the assorted light prints, cut *a total of*:

13 rectangles, 2½" x 12½"

11 rectangles, 2½" x 10½"

13 rectangles, 2½" x 8½"

11 rectangles, 2½" x 6½"

13 squares, 4½" x 4½"

From the assorted dark prints, cut *a total of*:

13 rectangles, 2½" x 12½"

24 rectangles, 2½" x 10½"

24 rectangles, 2½" x 8½"

24 rectangles, 2½" x 6½"

11 rectangles, 2½" x 4½"

13 squares, 4½" x 4½"

From the green print, cut:

7 strips, 2½" x 42"

Making the Blocks

Stitch all pieces with right sides together using a ¼" seam allowance.

This runner is assembled from 11 complete Log Cabin blocks and several different styles of partial blocks. Press each set of seam allowances away from the center square as you add new patches.

> ### LIGHT AND DARK
>
> Choose a variety of different fabrics for each block, but keep similar values together to create the characteristic light-and-shadow appearance of Log Cabin blocks.

BLOCK A

For variety, assemble some blocks by working clockwise around the center square, as shown in the illustrations on pages 8 and 9, and others by working counterclockwise around the center square.

1 Sew one dark 2½" x 4½" rectangle to the right edge of a light 4½" square. Stitch a dark 2½" x 6½" rectangle to the bottom of the unit.

2 Sew a light 2½" x 6½" rectangle to the left side of the unit. Stitch a light 2½" x 8½" rectangle to the top of the unit to complete the first round.

3 Sew a dark 2½" x 8½" rectangle to the right side of the unit. Stitch a dark 2½" x 10½" rectangle to the bottom of the unit. Notice that you are always adding light to light and dark to dark.

4 Sew a light 2½" x 10½" rectangle to the left side of the unit and a light 2½" x 12½" rectangle to the top of the unit to finish block A. Make 11.

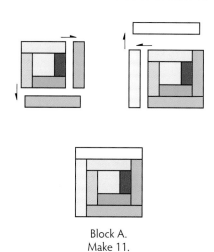

Block A.
Make 11.

BLOCK B

1 On the wrong side, mark the centers of a dark 2½" x 12½" rectangle, a dark 2½" x 8½" rectangle, and a dark 4½" square.

2 Aligning the center marks, sew the 2½" x 8½" rectangle to one side of the square. Stitch the 2½" x 12½" rectangle to the other side of the 2½" x 8½" rectangle with the center marks aligned to make block B. Make two.

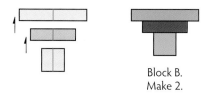

Block B.
Make 2.

BLOCK C

1 Stitch a dark 2½" x 6½" rectangle to the top of a light 4½" square as shown. Sew a light 2½" x 8½" rectangle to the right edge of the unit.

2 Sew a dark 2½" x 10½" rectangle to the top of the unit and stitch a light 2½" x 12½" rectangle to the right edge of the unit to make one block C.

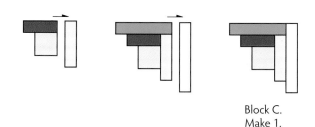

Block C.
Make 1.

BLOCK D

1 Stitch a dark 2½" x 6½" rectangle to the top of a light 4½" square as shown. Sew a light 2½" x 8½" rectangle to the left edge of the unit.

2 Sew a dark 2½" x 10½" rectangle to the top of the unit and a light 2½" x 12½" rectangle to the left edge of the unit to make one block D.

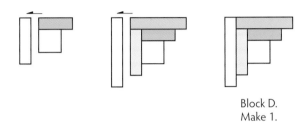

Block D.
Make 1.

BLOCK E

1 Stitch a dark 2½" x 6½" rectangle to the top of a dark 4½" square as shown. Sew a dark 2½" x 8½" rectangle to the right edge of the unit.

2 Sew a dark 2½" x 10½" rectangle to the top of the unit and a dark 2½" x 12½" rectangle to the right edge of the unit to make block E. Make 11.

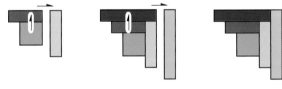

Block E.
Make 11.

Assembling the Bed Runner

1 Arrange the blocks as shown below, noting the orientation of each block.

2 Sew the blocks together in diagonal rows. Press the seam allowances in alternating directions from row to row. Join the rows to complete the runner top and press the seam allowances in one direction.

3 Trim the runner top to measure 25" x 102", squaring the corners.

Finishing the Bed Runner

For more information on any of the following steps, download free illustrated instructions at ShopMartingale.com/HowtoQuilt.

1 Cut the backing fabric to measure 31" x 108". Layer and baste the backing, batting, and bed-runner top.

2 Quilt as desired. The sample is quilted with an overall pattern of leaves, vines, and berries.

3 Trim the backing and batting even with the runner top.

4 Using the green 2½"-wide strips, bind the edges of the bed runner.

Runner assembly

White Diamonds

*Inspiration comes from everywhere—including floors!
Kimberly saw an interesting tile pattern on the floor of a hotel
lobby and turned it into a clean and crisp bed runner.*

Designed by Kimberly Jolly of Fat Quarter Shop, pieced by Tricia Poolson, and quilted by Diane Selman

FINISHED SIZE: 30½" x 100¼"

Materials

Yardage is based on 42"-wide fabric. The bed runner shown was made using the Bella Solids fabric collection by Moda Fabrics.

3¼ yards of white solid for blocks and border

1¼ yards of blue solid for blocks and binding

3 yards of fabric for backing

36" x 106" piece of batting

Cutting

From the white solid, cut:

1 strip, 11" x 42"; crosscut into 16 rectangles,
  2¼" x 11"

3 strips, 9¼" x 42"; crosscut 1 strip into
  16 rectangles, 2¼" x 9¼"

1 strip, 12¾" x 42"; crosscut into 10 rectangles,
  2¼" x 12¾"

2 strips, 7½" x 42"

2 strips, 2¼" x 42"

2 strips, 5¾" x 42"

2 strips, 4" x 42"

6 strips, 2⅜" x 42"

From the blue solid, cut:

8 strips, 2¼" x 42"; crosscut 2 strips into:
  21 squares, 2¼" x 2¼"
  4 rectangles, 2¼" x 5¾"

7 strips, 2½" x 42"

Making the Diamond Blocks

Stitch all pieces with right sides together using a ¼" seam allowance.

1 Sew a white 9¼" x 42" strip to a blue 2¼" x 42" strip to make strip set A. Press the seam allowances toward the blue strip. Make two. Crosscut the strip sets into 2¼"-wide segments; make 32 A segments.

2¼"

Strip set A.
Make 2 strip sets. Cut 32 segments.

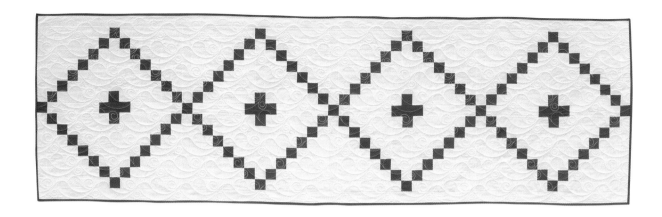

2 Sew a blue 2¼" x 42" strip between a white 7½" x 42" strip and a white 2¼" x 42" strip to make strip set B. Press the seam allowances toward the blue strip. Make two. Crosscut the strip sets into 2¼"-wide segments; make 32 B segments.

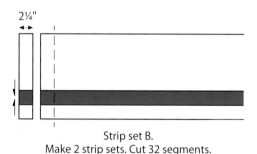

Strip set B.
Make 2 strip sets. Cut 32 segments.

3 Sew a blue 2¼" x 42" strip between a white 5¾" x 42" strip and a white 4" x 42" strip to make strip set C. Press the seam allowances toward the blue strip. Make two. Crosscut the strip sets into 2¼"-wide segments; make 32 C segments.

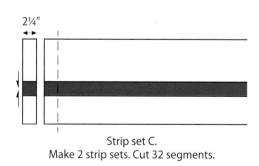

Strip set C.
Make 2 strip sets. Cut 32 segments.

4 Arrange two each of segments A, B, and C, rotating segments as shown. Stitch the segments together to make a quarter unit measuring 11" x 11". Press the seam allowances in one direction. Make 16.

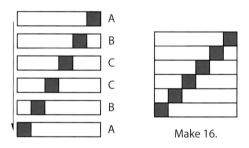

Make 16.

5 Sew a white 2¼" x 9¼" rectangle to a blue square to make a 2¼" x 11" sashing unit. Press the seam allowances toward the square. Make eight.

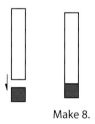

Make 8.

6 Sew a sashing unit between two quarter units, rotating one quarter unit as shown, to make a half unit measuring 11" x 23¼". Press the seam allowances toward the quarter units. Make eight.

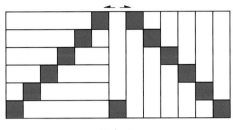

Make 8.

7 Sew a blue square between two white 2¼" x 11" rectangles to make a 2¼" x 23¼" outer-sashing unit. Press the seam allowances toward the blue square. Make eight.

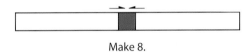

Make 8.

8 Sew a blue 2¼" x 5¾" rectangle between two white 2¼" x 9¼" rectangles to make a 2¼" x 23¼" center-sashing unit. Press the seam allowances toward the blue rectangle. Make four.

Make 4.

9 Stitch a center-sashing unit between two half units from step 6. Sew outer-sashing units to the top and bottom of the assembled unit to make a diamond block. Press the seam allowances away from the center-sashing unit. Make four.

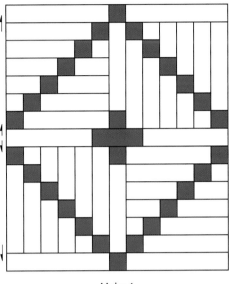

Make 4.

Assembling the Bed Runner

1 Sew a blue square between two white 2¼" x 12¾" rectangles to make a 2¼" x 26¾" vertical sashing strip. Press the seam allowances toward the blue square. Make five.

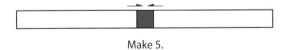

Make 5.

2 Lay out the diamond blocks and vertical sashing strips as shown on page 14. Sew the units together to make the runner center. Press the seam allowances toward the sashing.

3 Join the six white 2⅜" x 42" strips to make a long strip. Crosscut the long strip into two border strips, 2⅜" x 100¼". Sew the borders to the top and bottom of the runner center. Press the seam allowances toward the border.

Finishing the Bed Runner

For more information on any of the following steps, download free illustrated instructions at ShopMartingale.com/HowtoQuilt.

1 Cut the backing fabric to measure 36" x 106". Layer and baste the backing, batting, and bed-runner top.

2 Quilt as desired. The sample is quilted with swirls and petal motifs.

3 Trim the backing and batting even with the runner top.

4 Using the blue 2½"-wide strips, bind the edges of the bed runner.

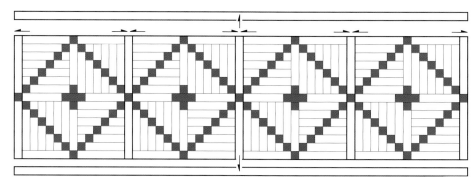

Runner assembly

Zen Chic

A limited color palette and simple repeated shapes give a soothing charm to this modern bed runner.

By Brigitte Heitland

//

FINISHED SIZE: 27½" x 92½"

Materials

Yardage is based on 42"-wide fabric. The bed runner shown was made using the Figures fabric collection by Brigitte Heitland for Moda Fabrics.

2½ yards of white solid for background
⅞ yard of bright-blue floral for triangles and binding
⅜ yard of light numbers print for triangles
⅜ yard of dark numbers print for triangles
⅜ yard of blue-on-white floral for triangles
⅜ yard of light floral for triangles
⅜ yard of dark floral for triangles
⅜ yard of dark circle print for triangles
⅜ yard of light cross print for triangles
⅜ yard of dark cross print for triangles
2¾ yards of fabric for backing
33" x 98" piece of batting

Cutting

From the light numbers print, cut:
2 strips, 5" x 42"; crosscut into:
    1 rectangle, 3½" x 5"
    8 rectangles, 4½" x 5"
    7 rectangles, 5" x 5½"

From the dark numbers print, cut:
2 strips, 5" x 42"; crosscut into:
    4 rectangles, 3½" x 5"
    9 rectangles, 4½" x 5"
    3 rectangles, 5" x 5½"

From the blue-on-white floral, cut:
2 strips, 5" x 42"; crosscut into:
    7 rectangles, 3½" x 5"
    8 rectangles, 4½" x 5"
    1 rectangle, 5" x 5½"

From the light floral, cut:
2 strips, 5" x 42"; crosscut into:
    4 rectangles, 3½" x 5"
    9 rectangles, 4½" x 5"
    3 rectangles, 5" x 5½"

From the bright-blue floral, cut:
2 strips, 5" x 42"; crosscut into:
    4 rectangles, 3½" x 5"
    8 rectangles, 4½" x 5"
    4 rectangles, 5½" x 5"
7 strips, 2½" x 42"

From the dark floral, cut:
2 strips, 5" x 42"; crosscut into:
    5 rectangles, 3½" x 5"
    8 rectangles, 4½" x 5"
    3 rectangles, 5" x 5½"

From the dark circle print, cut:
2 strips, 5" x 42"; crosscut into:
    6 rectangles, 3½" x 5"
    8 rectangles, 4½" x 5"
    2 rectangles, 5" x 5½"

Continued on page 17

Continued from page 15

From the light cross print, cut:
2 strips, 5" x 42"; crosscut into:
    5 rectangles, 3½" x 5"
    10 rectangles, 4½" x 5"
    1 rectangle, 5" x 5½"

From the dark cross print, cut:
2 strips, 5" x 42"; crosscut into:
    12 rectangles, 3½" x 5"
    4 rectangles, 4½" x 5"

From the white solid, cut:
10 strips, 4" x 42", plus additional strips as needed

Making the Units

Stitch all pieces with right sides together using a ¼" seam allowance. The height of the triangles will always be 5", regardless of their width.

1 Place a quilter's ruler on the right side of a print 4½" x 5" rectangle at an angle, positioning the ruler so that its ¼" line bisects the lower-right corner of the print rectangle. Trim the print rectangle along the ruler's edge. Lay the trimmed rectangle on a white strip, matching the raw edges and making sure that the white strip will extend far enough to complete the 4½" x 5" rectangle when the unit is pressed open.

2 Stitch a ¼" seam along the trimmed edge of the rectangle. Check the placement of the white

fabric, and then flip the white fabric into position and press the seam allowances open.

3 Align a ruler with the straight edges of the print rectangle, positioning the 4½" marking along the side edge. Trim the excess white strip so that the unit measures 4½" x 5", the same size as the original rectangle.

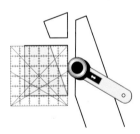

4 On the wrong side of the unit, mark a seamline from the lower-right corner to the top edge, intersecting the previous seam ¼" from the top of the unit.

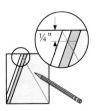

5 Trim the print fabric ¼" outside the marked line. Align the edge of the white strip with the newly cut edge and stitch on the marked line. Press the seam allowances open. Trim the unit to measure 4½" x 5" again.

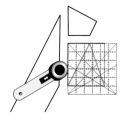

6 Repeat steps 1–5 to make 72 medium units (4½" x 5"), 48 small units (3½" x 5"), and 24 large units (5" x 5½"). Start a new white strip when the current one becomes too small to use, and cut more white strips as necessary.

3½"	4½"	5½"

Small unit.
Make 48.

Medium unit.
Make 72.

Large unit.
Make 24.

Assembling the Panels

This bed runner is assembled in panels labeled A and B. Press all seam allowances open.

1 Choosing a variety of print fabrics, join six units in the order shown to make panel A. Make 13.

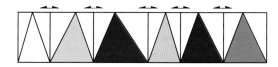

Panel A.
Make 13.

2 Again, choosing a variety of prints, join six units as shown to make panel B. Make 11.

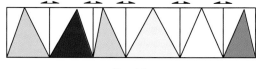

Panel B.
Make 11.

Assembling the Bed Runner

1 Referring to the assembly diagram below, arrange the panels in six rows of four panels each.

2 Sew the panels together in rows. Join the rows to complete the bed runner.

WONKY WORKS!

While joining the rows, you won't always get a sharp point at the tip of each triangle. Don't worry—you didn't do anything wrong. Because the angles aren't all 45°, it's not always possible to achieve a sharp point. This is part of the improvisational piecing, so just go with it!

Finishing the Bed Runner

For more information on any of the following steps, download free illustrated instructions at ShopMartingale.com/HowtoQuilt.

1 Cut the backing fabric to measure 33" x 98". Layer and baste the backing, batting, and bed-runner top.

2 Quilt as desired. The sample is machine quilted with a small-scale design in the white triangles, leaving the print fabrics unquilted.

3 Trim the batting and backing even with the runner top.

4 Using the bright-blue floral 2½"-wide strips, bind the edges of the bed runner.

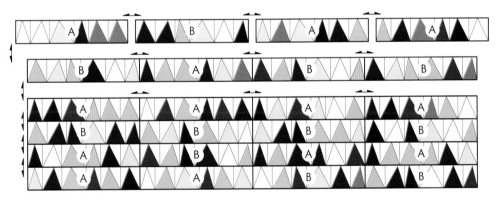

Runner assembly

Burst

Imagine what would happen if a traditional quilt block burst apart on your bed. This cheerful runner seems to capture the outcome.

By Megan Jimenez of Quilt Story

//

FINISHED SIZE: 29½" x 96½"

Materials

Yardage is based on 42"-wide fabric. The bed runner shown was made using the Oval Elements fabric collection by Art Gallery Fabrics and white solid by Kona Cottons for Robert Kaufman Fabrics.

2¼ yards of white solid for blocks and sashing

½ yard of purple print for blocks

½ yard of aqua print for blocks

½ yard of teal print for blocks

½ yard of blue print for blocks

⅓ yard of green print for blocks

⅝ yard of red print for binding

2⅞ yards of fabric for backing

35" x 102" piece of batting

Cutting

From the white solid, cut:

1 strip, 6½" x 42"; crosscut into 4 squares, 6½" x 6½"

6 strips, 4" x 42"; crosscut into 60 squares, 4" x 4"*

10 strips, 3½" x 42"; crosscut 6 strips into:
   8 squares, 3½" x 3½"
   20 rectangles, 3½" x 6½"
   4 rectangles, 3½" x 9½"

5 strips, 1½" x 42"*

*If your fabric is narrow, you may need to cut an additional strip.

From the purple print, cut:

2 strips, 3½" x 42"; crosscut into 16 squares, 3½" x 3½"

2 strips, 4" x 42"; crosscut into 16 squares, 4" x 4"

From the teal print, cut:

1 strip, 3½" x 42"; crosscut into 12 squares, 3½" x 3½"*

2 strips, 4" x 42"; crosscut into 12 squares, 4" x 4"

From the blue print, cut:

1 strip, 3½" x 42"; crosscut into 12 squares, 3½" x 3½"*

2 strips, 4" x 42"; crosscut into 12 squares, 4" x 4"

From the aqua print, cut:

1 strip, 3½" x 42"; crosscut into 12 squares, 3½" x 3½"*

2 strips, 4" x 42"; crosscut into 12 squares, 4" x 4"

From the green print, cut:

1 strip, 3½" x 42"; crosscut into 8 squares, 3½" x 3½"

1 strip, 4" x 42"; crosscut into 8 squares, 4" x 4"

From the red print, cut:

7 strips, 2½" x 42"

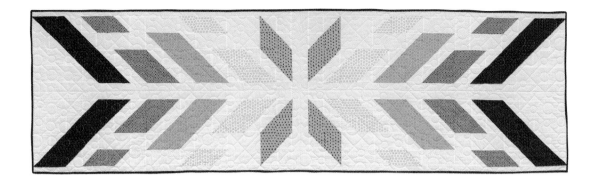

Making the Half-Square-Triangle Units

Stitch all pieces with right sides together using a ¼" seam allowance.

1 Draw a diagonal line from corner to corner on the wrong side of each white 4" square. Place a marked square on a purple 4" square, right sides together, and sew ¼" from both sides of the drawn line. Cut on the drawn line and press the seam allowances toward the purple triangles to make two half-square-triangle units. Trim the units to measure 3½" x 3½". Make 32.

Make 32.

2 Repeat step 1 using marked white squares with the teal, blue, and aqua 4" squares to make 24 half-square-triangle units of each color combination. Repeat again to make 16 units using the remaining marked white squares with the green 4" squares.

Make 24.

Make 24.

Make 24.

Make 16.

BLENDING BLOCKS

Choose fabrics with subtle prints to disguise the seamlines in the finished bed runner.

Making the Blocks

Stitch all pieces with right sides together using a ¼" seam allowance. While not assembled in traditional pieced blocks, this runner is made up of pieced units that we'll refer to as blocks A–E. Be aware that the units are different sizes. You'll also need to make some of the blocks in a second, mirror-image configuration.

BLOCK A

1 Arrange two green half-square-triangle units with a green 3½" square, a white 3½" square, and a white 6½" square as shown. Sew the units and squares together, pressing the seam allowances toward the squares.

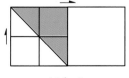

Make 2.

2 Lay out two green half-square-triangle units, one green 3½" square, three aqua half-square-triangle units, and two aqua 3½" squares as shown. Stitch the units together in rows, pressing the seam allowances in opposite directions from row to row. Join the rows and press the seam allowances in one direction.

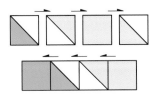 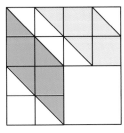

Make 2.

3 Sew the units from steps 1 and 2 together to complete block A1. Make two. Repeat, reversing the layout of the units, to make two of block A2.

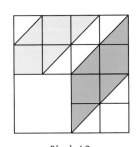

Block A1.
Make 2.

Block A2.
Make 2.

BLOCK B

1 Sew a blue half-square-triangle unit to a blue 3½" square and press the seam allowances toward the blue square.

2 Stitch a white 3½" x 6½" rectangle to the top of the unit and press the seam allowances toward the white rectangle. Sew a second white 3½" x 6½" rectangle to one side of the unit and press the seam allowances toward the white rectangle.

  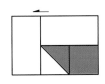

Make 2.

3 Arrange two blue half-square-triangle units, two purple half-square-triangle units, and one each of the blue and purple 3½" squares as shown. Stitch the units together in rows, pressing the seam allowances in opposite directions from row to row. Join the rows and press the seam allowances in one direction.

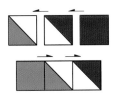 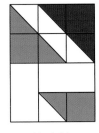

4 Sew the units from steps 2 and 3 together to complete block B1. Make two. Repeat, reversing the layout of the units, to make two of block B2.

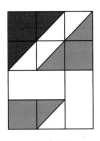

Block B1.
Make 2.

Block B2.
Make 2.

BLOCK C

1 Lay out two blue half-square-triangle units, one blue 3½" square, four teal half-square-triangle units, two teal 3½" squares, one aqua half-square-triangle unit, and one white 3½" x 6½" rectangle as shown. Sew the units together in rows. Press the seam allowances in opposite directions from row to row.

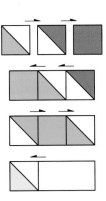

2 Join the rows to make block C1. Press the seam allowances in one direction. Make two. Repeat, reversing the layout of the units, to make two of block C2.

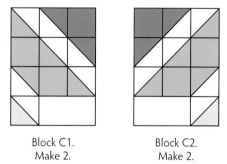

Block C1.
Make 2.

Block C2.
Make 2.

2 Join the rows to make block D1. Press the seam allowances in one direction. Make two. Repeat steps 1–3, reversing the layout of the units, to make two of block D2.

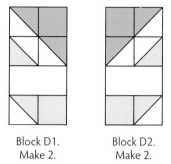

Block D1.
Make 2.

Block D2.
Make 2.

BLOCK D

1 Lay out two teal half-square-triangle units, one teal 3½" square, two aqua half-square-triangle units, one aqua 3½" square, and one white 3½" x 6½" rectangle as shown. Sew the units together in rows. Press the seam allowances in opposite directions from row to row.

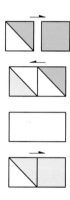

BLOCK E

1 Arrange six purple half-square-triangle units, three purple 3½" squares, one blue half-square-triangle unit, one white 3½" square, one white 3½" x 9½" rectangle, and one white 3½" x 6½" rectangle as shown. Sew the units together in rows. Press the seam allowances in opposite directions from row to row.

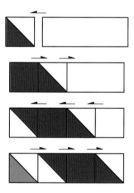

2 Join the rows to make block E. Press the seam allowances in one direction. Make four.

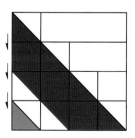

Block E.
Make 4.

Assembling the Bed Runner

1 Lay out one each of blocks A1, B1, C1, D1, and E as shown. Sew the blocks together to make a 12½" x 48½" quarter section. Make two.

Quarter section.
Make 2.

2 Arrange one each of blocks A2, B2, C2, D2, and E as shown. Sew the blocks together to make a 12½" x 48½" reversed quarter section. Make two.

Reversed quarter section.
Make 2.

3 Sew the short ends of three white 3½" x 42" strips together to make a long strip. Crosscut the long strip into two 48½" lengths.

4 Sew one 48½"-long strip between a quarter section and a reversed quarter section as shown on page 26. Press the seam allowances toward the white strip. Make two.

5 Sew the short ends of the white 1½" x 42" strips together to make a long strip. Crosscut the long strip into four 48½" lengths.

6 Sew white 1½" x 48½" strips to the top and bottom of each unit from step 4. Press the seam allowances toward the white strips.

Make 2.

7 Trim the remaining white 3½" x 42" strip to a 29½" length. Sew the strip between the two sections and press the seam allowances toward the strip to complete the runner top.

Finishing the Bed Runner

For more information on any of the following steps, download free illustrated instructions at ShopMartingale.com/HowtoQuilt.

1 Cut the backing fabric to measure 35" x 102". Layer and baste the backing, batting, and bed-runner top.

2 Quilt as desired. The sample is quilted with an overall pattern of circles and lines.

3 Trim the backing and batting even with the runner top.

4 Using the red-print 2½"-wide strips, bind the edges of the bed runner.

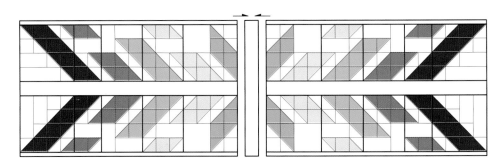

Runner assembly

Summertime

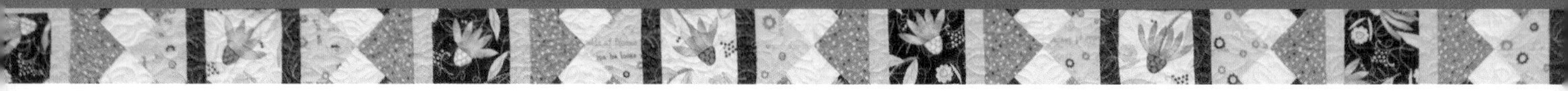

Peekaboo Daisy

A pair of coordinating daisy prints peek from the centers of pieced stars in this lively bed runner. Look closely— the design creates a secondary X-shaped pattern, too.

By Heidi Pridemore

FINISHED SIZE: 26½" x 98½"

Materials

Yardage is based on 42"-wide fabric. The bed runner shown was made using the One for You, One for Me fabric collection by Pat Sloan for Moda Fabrics.

1⅛ yards of cream solid for blocks

⅞ yard of orange dot for blocks

⅞ yard of red dot for blocks and binding

⅝ yard of green floral for blocks

⅜ yard of green swirl print for blocks

⅜ yard of red swirl print for blocks

⅜ yard of green dot for border

⅓ yard of red floral for blocks

⅓ yard of orange swirl print for blocks

¼ yard of red large-scale floral for block centers

¼ yard of cream large-scale floral for block centers

3 yards of fabric for backing

32" x 104" piece of batting

Cutting

From the cream solid, cut:

4 strips, 4¼" x 42"; crosscut into 32 squares, 4¼" x 4¼". Cut each square into quarters diagonally to make 128 small triangles.

4 strips, 3⅞" x 42"; crosscut into 32 squares, 3⅞" x 3⅞"

From the red dot, cut:

2 strips, 3⅞" x 42"; crosscut into 16 squares, 3⅞" x 3⅞"

7 strips, 2½" x 42"

From the orange dot, cut:

2 strips, 4¼" x 42"; crosscut into 16 squares, 4¼" x 4¼". Cut each square into quarters diagonally to make 64 small triangles.

4 strips, 3⅞" x 42"; crosscut into 32 squares, 3⅞" x 3⅞". Cut each square in half diagonally to make 64 large triangles.

From the green floral, cut:

4 strips, 3⅞" x 42"; crosscut into 32 squares, 3⅞" x 3⅞". Cut each square in half diagonally to make 64 large triangles.

From the red swirl print, cut:

1 strip, 4½" x 42"; crosscut into 16 rectangles, 1½" x 4½"

1 strip, 6½" x 42"; crosscut into 16 rectangles, 1½" x 6½"

From the cream large-scale floral, cut:

1 strip, 4½" x 42"; crosscut into 8 squares, 4½" x 4½"

From the orange swirl print, cut:

2 strips, 3⅞" x 42"; crosscut into 16 squares, 3⅞" x 3⅞"

From the red floral, cut:

2 strips, 4¼" x 42"; crosscut into 16 squares, 4¼" x 4¼". Cut each square into quarters diagonally to make 64 small triangles.

Continued on page 30

Continued from page 28

From the green swirl print, cut:
1 strip, 4½" x 42"; crosscut into 16 rectangles,
   1½" x 4½"
1 strip, 6½" x 42"; crosscut into 16 rectangles,
   1½" x 6½"

From the red large-scale floral, cut:
1 strip, 4½" x 42"; crosscut into 8 squares,
   4½" x 4½"

From the green dot, cut:
2 strips, 1½" x 24½"
5 strips, 1½" x 42"

PREVIEW IT

To find a large-scale print suitable for the center squares, make a window template: cut a 6" square from cardstock and then cut a 4" square from its center, creating a window. Place the template on the fabric to see what portion of the print will be revealed in the finished block.

Making Block A

Stitch all pieces with right sides together using a ¼" seam allowance.

1 Draw a diagonal line from corner to corner on the wrong side of each cream 3⅞" square. Set 16 aside for block B.

2 Place a marked cream square on a red-dot 3⅞" square with right sides together. Sew ¼" from both sides of the drawn line. Cut on the drawn line to make two half-square-triangle units and press the seam allowances toward the red triangle. Make four.

Make 4.

3 Sew a small orange-dot triangle to a small cream triangle, orienting the pieces as shown. Press the seam allowances toward the orange triangle. Stitch the pieced triangle to a large green-floral triangle to make a left unit. Press the seam allowances toward the green triangle. Make four.

Left unit.
Make 4.

4 Repeat step 3, changing the placement as shown, to make a right unit. Make four.

Right unit.
Make 4.

5 Sew a left unit to each right unit as shown to make a side unit. Press the seam allowances to one side. Make four.

Side unit.
Make 4.

6 Sew red-swirl 1½" x 4½" rectangles to opposite sides of a cream floral square. Press the seam allowances toward the red rectangles. Sew red-swirl 1½" x 6½" rectangles to the top and bottom of the unit to make the center unit. Press the seam allowances toward the red rectangles.

Center unit.
Make 1.

7 Arrange the center, side, and half-square-triangle units as shown. Sew the units together in rows, pressing the seam allowances in opposite directions from row to row. Join the rows to complete block A. Press the seam allowances in one direction. Make eight blocks, 12½" x 12½".

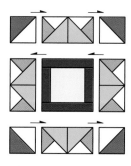 

Block A.
Make 8.

Making Block B

Block B is assembled in the same way as block A, but with different color placement. Refer to the previous instructions and illustrations as you assemble block B.

1 Sew the remaining marked cream squares to orange-swirl squares to make half-square-triangle units. Make four.

2 Make left and right units as before, using the small red-floral triangles, small cream triangles, and the large orange-dot triangles. Make four left and four right units.

3 Sew a left unit to a right unit to make a side unit. Make four.

4 Sew green-swirl 1½" x 4½" rectangles to opposite sides of a red large-scale floral square. Sew green-swirl 1½" x 6½" rectangles to the top and bottom of the unit to make the center unit.

5 Arrange and stitch the units as shown to complete block B. Make eight, each measuring 12½" x 12½".

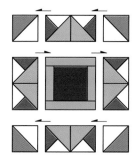 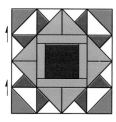

Block B.
Make 8.

Assembling the Bed Runner

1 Arrange the blocks, alternating the A and B blocks, in two rows of eight blocks each.

2 Sew the blocks together in rows. Press the seam allowances to the right in one row and to the left in the other. Join the rows to complete the runner center, pressing the seam allowances to one side.

3 Sew a green-dot 1½" x 24½" strip to each end of the quilt center. Press the seam allowances toward the border.

4 Sew the five remaining green-dot strips together to make a long strip. Crosscut the strip into two borders, 1½" x 98½". Sew these borders to the top and bottom of the runner center. Press the seam allowances toward the border.

Finishing the Bed Runner

For more information on any of the following steps, download free illustrated instructions at ShopMartingale.com/HowtoQuilt.

1 Cut the backing fabric to measure 32" x 104". Layer and baste the backing, batting, and bed-runner top.

2 Quilt as desired. The sample is quilted with a meandering overall pattern of leaves.

3 Trim the backing and batting even with the runner top.

4 Using the red-dot 2½"-wide strips, bind the edges of the bed runner.

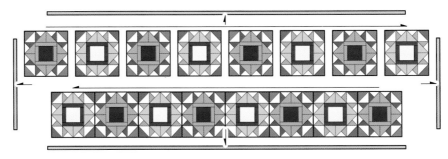

Runner assembly

Art Gallery

Whether you view it as a single work of art or a line of paintings on a gallery wall, the design of this bed runner puts your sense of color and style on display for all to see.

By Amanda Leins

FINISHED SIZE: 28½" x 100½"

Materials

Yardage is based on 42"-wide fabric. The bed runner shown was made using various fabrics by Art Gallery Fabrics.

1⅛ yards of white solid for blocks

¾ yard of light-rose tone on tone for blocks

⅝ yard of white floral for blocks

½ yard of light-orange tone on tone for blocks

⅓ yard of light-green tone on tone for blocks

⅝ yard of dark-blue solid for binding

3 yards of fabric for backing

34" x 106" piece of batting

VALUABLE ADVICE

Choose a floral print that falls between the white background and the light-rose tone on tone to bridge their values and give the bed runner an artistic blend of color and texture.

Cutting

From the white floral, cut:
1 strip, 12½" x 42"; crosscut into 8 rectangles,
   4½" x 12½"
1 strip, 4½" x 42"; crosscut into 6 squares,
   4½" x 4½"

From the light-green tone on tone, cut:
2 strips, 4½" x 42"; crosscut into:
   14 squares, 4½" x 4½"
   3 rectangles, 2½" x 4½"

From the light-rose tone on tone, cut:
5 strips, 4½" x 42"; crosscut into:
   8 rectangles, 4½" x 12½"
   4 rectangles, 4½" x 8½"
   8 squares, 4½" x 4½"

From the white solid, cut:
4 strips, 4½" x 42"; crosscut into:
   20 squares, 4½" x 4½"
   2 rectangles, 4½" x 28½"
2 strips, 8½" x 42"; crosscut into 6 rectangles,
   8½" x 12½"

From the light-orange tone on tone, cut:
1 strip, 12½" x 42"; crosscut into:
   6 rectangles, 4½" x 12½"
   6 rectangles, 1½" x 4½"

From the dark-blue solid, cut:
7 strips, 2½" x 42"

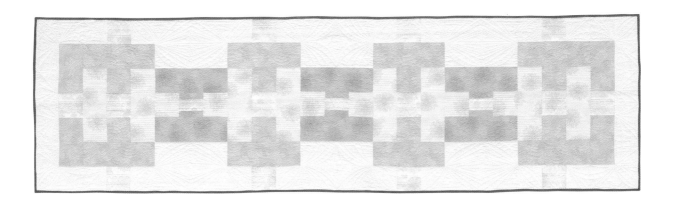

Making Row A

For all rows, stitch all pieces with right sides together using a ¼" seam allowance.

1 Sew a light-green 4½" square between two light-rose 4½" squares to make a center unit. Press the seam allowances toward the light-rose squares.

2 Sew a white-floral 4½" x 12½" rectangle to each long edge of the center unit. Press the seam allowances toward the floral rectangles.

3 Stitch light-rose 4½" x 12½" rectangles to the top and bottom of the center unit. Press the seam allowances toward the light-rose rectangles.

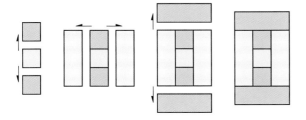

4 Sew a light-green 4½" square between two white 4½" squares to make a three-square unit. Press the seam allowances toward the light-green square. Make two.

5 Sew the three-square units to the top and bottom of the center unit to complete row A, which should measure 12½" x 28½". Press the seam allowances toward the light-rose rectangles. Make four of row A.

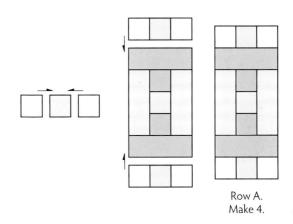

Row A.
Make 4.

Making Row B

1 Sew a light-green 2½" x 4½" rectangle between two light-orange 1½" x 4½" rectangles to make a square unit. Press the seam allowances toward the light-green rectangle.

2 Sew a white-floral 4½" square to each side of the pieced square to make a center unit. Press the seam allowances toward the floral squares.

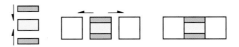

3 Sew light-orange 4½" x 12½" rectangles to the top and bottom of the center unit. Press the seam allowances toward the light-orange rectangles.

4 Sew white 8½" x 12½" rectangles to the top and bottom of the center unit to complete row B, which will measure 12½" x 28½". Press the seam allowances toward the light-orange rectangles. Make three of row B.

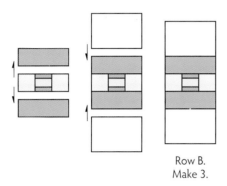

Row B.
Make 3.

Making Row C

1 Sew a light-green 4½" square between two light-rose 4½" x 8½" rectangles. Press the seam allowances toward the light-rose rectangles.

2 Sew white 4½" squares to the top and bottom of the three-patch unit. Press the seam allowances toward the white squares.

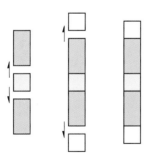

3 Stitch a white 4½" x 28½" rectangle to one long edge of the unit to complete row C, which will measure 8½" x 28½". Press the seam allowances toward the white rectangle. Make two of row C.

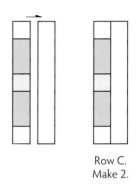

Row C.
Make 2.

Assembling the Bed Runner

1 Arrange the A, B, and C rows as shown. Rotate one of the C rows to match the diagram.

2 Stitch the rows together to complete the runner top. Press the seam allowances in one direction.

Runner assembly

Finishing the Bed Runner

For more information on any of the following steps, download free illustrated instructions at ShopMartingale.com/HowtoQuilt.

1 Cut the backing fabric to measure 34" x 106". Layer and baste the backing, batting, and bed-runner top.

2 Quilt as desired. The sample is quilted with a combination of patterns including parallel lines, fanned lines, and overlapping concentric circles to add variety and define individual areas of the runner.

3 Trim the backing and batting even with the runner top.

4 Using the dark-blue 2½"-wide strips, bind the edges of the bed runner.

Vintage Petal

The curvy petals in this cute runner are appliquéd, so there's no tricky curved piecing to slow you down. A linen background gives the bed runner its retro appeal.

By Heather Andrus and Megan Jimenez of Quilt Story

FINISHED SIZE: 24½" x 96½"

Materials

Yardage is based on 42"-wide fabric. The bed runner shown was made using the Flower Sugar fabric collection by Lecien.

2¼ yards of linen or linen/cotton blend for blocks

⅛ yard *each* of 10 assorted prints *OR* assorted scraps totaling 1¼ yards for appliqués

⅝ yard of red print for binding

2⅞ yards of fabric for backing

30" x 102" piece of batting

4⅜ yards of ¾"-wide cotton crocheted lace

Paper-backed fusible web

Appliqué glue

Fabric starch

FABULOUS LINEN

Before cutting, heavily starch and iron the linen fabric to give it body and reduce fraying. Prewash *all* of the fabrics; you'll need to wash the project after it's finished to remove the starch. The cotton crocheted lace should be prewashed or soaked first as well, to make sure it won't shrink.

Cutting

From the linen or linen/cotton blend, cut:
36 squares, 8½" x 8½"

From the ¾"-wide lace, cut:
18 strips, 8½" long

From the red print, cut:
7 strips, 2½" x 42"

Preparing the Appliqués

Trace 72 petals (page 40) onto the paper side of the fusible web, leaving ½" between shapes. Roughly cut out each petal ¼" outside the line. Following the manufacturer's instructions, fuse the petals to the wrong side of the assorted prints. Cut out each appliqué shape on the drawn line.

Making the Petal Blocks

For all blocks, stitch all pieces with right sides together using a ¼" seam allowance.

1 Remove the paper backing from four petals cut from different fabrics. Arrange the petals on a linen square, making sure the petal points meet and leaving a ¼" seam allowance on all four sides of the linen square.

2 Use your favorite appliqué method to stitch the petals to the linen. Match thread colors to the appliqué fabrics, or use a neutral color throughout the project. Appliqués on the sample runner are attached with a straight machine stitch positioned close to the appliqué edges. Make 18 blocks, using four different fabrics for the petals in each block.

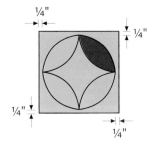

Make 18.

Making the Lace Blocks

1 Fold a linen square in half and press lightly to locate the centerline. Using appliqué glue, adhere an 8½"-long lace strip along the center of the square.

2 Edgestitch both long edges of the lace and then zigzag along the centerline of the lace, using thread that matches the lace. Make 18.

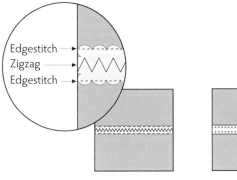

Make 18.

Assembling the Bed Runner

1 Arrange the petal and lace blocks in an alternating pattern as shown below.

2 Sew the blocks together in rows. Press the seam allowances toward the lace blocks.

3 Join the rows to complete the runner top and press the seam allowances to one side.

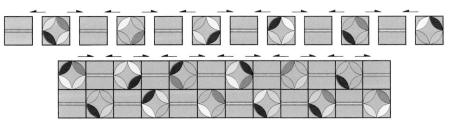

Runner assembly

Finishing the Bed Runner

For more information on any of the following steps, download free illustrated instructions at ShopMartingale.com/HowtoQuilt.

1 Cut the backing fabric to measure 30" x 102". Layer and baste the backing, batting, and bed-runner top.

2 Quilt as desired. The sample is quilted with a motif at the center of each petal circle and to each side of the lace strips.

3 Trim the backing and batting even with the runner top.

4 Using the red-print 2½"-wide strips, bind the edges of the bed runner.

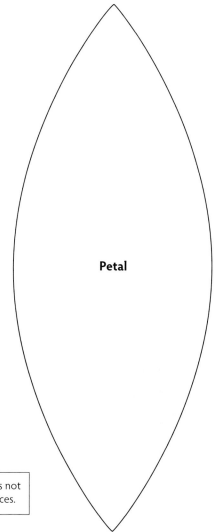

Petal

Appliqué pattern does not include seam allowances.

Hester's Crossing

This bed-runner design began with an idea for a small quilt with lots of tiny pieces. Jocelyn supersized the pattern, which resulted in the echoed diamonds, Xs, and the flowing ribbons of color.

Designed by Jocelyn Ueng of It's Sew Emma, pieced by Debbie Taylor, and quilted by Diane Selman

FINISHED SIZE: 26½" x 105½"

Materials

Yardage is based on 42"-wide fabric. The bed runner shown was made using the Pedal Pushers fabric collection by Lauren + Jessi Jung for Moda Fabrics.

1⅝ yards of white solid for blocks

1¼ yards of navy floral for blocks and binding

¾ yard of red floral for blocks

½ yard of blue print for blocks

½ yard of green print for blocks

⅓ yard of chevron stripe for blocks

⅓ yard of red print for blocks

¼ yard of pink print for blocks

¼ yard of yellow print for blocks

¼ yard of light-green print for border

3 yards of fabric for backing

32" x 111" piece of batting

Cutting

From the blue print, cut:
3 strips, 4" x 42"; crosscut into 24 squares, 4" x 4"

From the white solid, cut:
6 strips, 2¼" x 42"; crosscut into:
    24 rectangles, 2¼" x 4"
    24 rectangles, 2¼" x 5¾"
6 strips, 3" x 42"; crosscut into:
    4 rectangles, 3" x 11"
    4 rectangles, 3" x 21½"
    2 rectangles, 3" x 26½"
5 strips, 4" x 42"; crosscut into 24 rectangles,
    4" x 7½"

From the red floral, cut:
2 strips, 7½" x 42"; crosscut into 6 squares,
    7½" x 7½"
1 strip, 4" x 42"; crosscut into 6 squares, 4" x 4"
1 strip, 3" x 42"; crosscut into 3 rectangles, 3" x 11"

From the navy floral, cut:
2 strips, 7½" x 42"; crosscut into 6 squares,
    7½" x 7½"
1 strip, 4" x 42"; crosscut into 6 squares, 4" x 4"
1 strip, 3" x 42"; crosscut into 3 rectangles, 3" x 11"
7 strips, 2½" x 42"

From the green print, cut:
3 strips, 4" x 42"; crosscut into 24 squares, 4" x 4"

From the pink print, cut:
3 strips, 2¼" x 42"; crosscut into 48 squares,
    2¼" x 2¼"

From the chevron stripe, cut:
2 strips, 4" x 42"; crosscut into 12 squares, 4" x 4"

From the yellow print, cut:
3 strips, 2¼" x 42"; crosscut into 48 squares,
    2¼" x 2¼"

From the red print, cut:
2 strips, 4" x 42"; crosscut into 12 squares, 4" x 4"

From the light-green print, cut:
2 rectangles, 3¼" x 26½"

Making the Blue Star Blocks

For all blocks, stitch all pieces with right sides together using a ¼" seam allowance.

1 Draw a diagonal line from corner to corner on the wrong side of each blue 4" square. Place a marked square on the left end of a white 4" x 7½" rectangle as shown. Sew on the drawn line. Trim ¼" outside the seamline and press the seam allowances toward the corner to complete a left unit. Make six units.

2 Place a marked blue square on the right end of a white 4" x 7½" rectangle as shown and repeat step 1 to make a right unit. Make six units.

Make 6.   Make 6.

3 Place a marked blue square on the top-left corner of a red-floral 7½" square. Sew on the drawn line. Trim ¼" outside the seamline and press the seam allowances toward the corner. Stitch a second blue square to the bottom-right corner of the red-floral square to make a star center. Make three units.

Make 3.

4 Arrange a left unit, a red-floral 4" square, a star center, and a right unit as shown below. Sew the units together in rows. Join the rows to make a red quarter-star unit. Make three.

5 Repeat steps 3 and 4, substituting navy floral for the red 7½" and 4" squares. Make three navy quarter-star units.

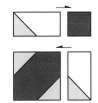

Make 3.   Make 3.

6 Sew a red quarter-star unit to the top of a navy quarter-star unit. Press the seam allowances to one side. Sew white 3" x 11" rectangles to the top and bottom of the unit to make a blue Half-Star block measuring 11" x 26½". Press the seam allowances toward the white rectangles.

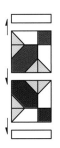 

Make 1.

7 Arrange the remaining quarter-star units as shown. Sew the units together in rows, pressing the seam allowances in opposite directions. Join the rows to make a square unit and press the seam allowances in one direction. Sew white 3" x 21½" rectangles to the top and bottom of the unit to make a blue Star block measuring 21½" x 26½".

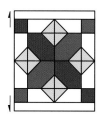 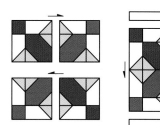

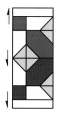

Make 1.

Making the Green Star Blocks

1 Follow the instructions for the blue Star block, substituting green 4" squares for the blue 4" squares, to make three red and three navy quarter-star units.

2 Arrange the units as shown to make one green Half-Star block and one green Star block.

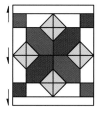

Make 1.   Make 1.

Making the Small-Star Blocks

1 Draw a diagonal line from corner to corner on the wrong side of each pink 2¼" square. Place a marked square on the right end of a white 2¼" x 5¾" rectangle as shown. Sew on the drawn line. Trim ¼" outside the seamline and press the seam allowances toward the corner to make a long right unit. Make six units.

2 Place a marked pink square on the left end of a white 2¼" x 5¾" rectangle and repeat step 1 to make a long left unit. Make six units.

Make 6.   Make 6.

3 Place a marked pink square on the right end of a white 2¼" x 4" rectangle as shown. Repeat step 1 to make a short right unit. Make six.

4 Place a marked pink square on the left end of a white 2¼" x 4" rectangle as shown and repeat step 1 to make a short left unit. Make six.

Make 6.   Make 6.

5 Place a marked pink square on the top-right corner of a chevron-stripe 4" square. Sew on the drawn line. Trim ¼" outside the seamline and press the seam allowances toward the corner. Stitch a second pink square to the bottom-left corner of the chevron-stripe square to make a star-center unit. Make 12.

Make 12.

6 Sew a short left unit to the side of a star-center unit as shown. Press the seam allowances toward the left unit. Stitch a long right unit to the top of the unit to make a left quarter-star unit. Make six.

Make 6.

7 Sew a short right unit to the side of a star-center unit as shown. Press the seam allowances toward the right unit. Stitch a long left unit to the top of the unit to make a right quarter-star unit. Make six.

Make 6.

8 Arrange two left and two right quarter-star units as shown. Sew the units together in rows, pressing the seam allowances in opposite directions. Join the rows to make a pink Small-Star block measuring 11" x 11". Press the seam allowances in one direction. Make three.

Make 3.

9 Repeat steps 1–8 to make three yellow Small-Star blocks, using the yellow 2¼" squares and red 4" squares.

Make 3.

10 Sew a pink Small-Star block to the top of a yellow Small-Star block and press the seam allowances to one side. Sew a red-floral 3" x 11" rectangle to the top of the unit and a navy-floral 3" x 11" rectangle to the bottom of the unit to make a small-star panel measuring 11" x 26½". Press the seam allowances toward the floral rectangles. Make three.

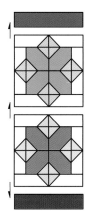 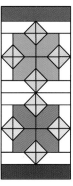

Make 3.

Assembling the Bed Runner

1 Arrange the panels, blocks, and half blocks as shown below. Sew the units together and press the seam allowances away from the center small-star panel.

2 Stitch a white 3" x 26½" rectangle to each end of the runner. Press the seam allowances toward the white rectangles.

3 Sew a light-green 3¼" x 26½" rectangle to each end of the runner. Press the seam allowances toward the light-green rectangles.

Finishing the Bed Runner

For more information on any of the following steps, download free illustrated instructions at ShopMartingale.com/HowtoQuilt.

1 Cut the backing fabric to measure 32" x 111". Layer and baste the backing, batting, and bed-runner top.

2 Quilt as desired. The sample is quilted with rows of curving feathers.

3 Trim the backing and batting even with the runner top.

4 Using the navy-floral 2½"-wide strips, bind the edges of the bed runner.

Runner assembly

Rich and Earthy

Solitaire

Diamonds are forever in this evocative bed runner. The crisp black-and-white palette with a pop of muted red makes this a sophisticated design you're sure to "bond" with.

By Stephanie Prescott

FINISHED SIZE: 32½" x 80½"

Materials

Yardage is based on 42"-wide fabric. Fat quarters are approximately 18" x 21". The bed runner shown was made using the Hot Off the Press fabric collection by Stephanie Prescott for Fresh Water Designs with E.E. Schenck Company.

1 fat quarter *each* of 7 assorted black-and-white prints for blocks

1 fat quarter *each* of 2 red prints for blocks

1⅝ yards of white solid for blocks

½ yard of black-and-red print for binding

2½ yards of fabric for backing

38" x 86" piece of batting

Cutting

From the assorted black-and-white prints, *cut a total of:*
16 rectangles, 5¼" x 18"

From the white solid, cut:
8 strips, 5¼" x 42"; crosscut into 16 rectangles, 5¼" x 18"
1 strip, 9¼" x 42"; crosscut into 2 rectangles, 9¼" x 18"

From *each* of the red prints, cut:
1 rectangle, 9¼" x 18" (2 total)

From the black-and-red print, cut:
6 strips, 2½" x 42"

Making the Small Units

Stitch all pieces with right sides together using a ¼" seam allowance.

1 Place a black-and-white rectangle on a white 5¼" x 18" rectangle with right sides together. Measure and mark ½" from the top-left and bottom-right corners. Cut the stacked rectangles in half from mark to mark as shown. Repeat to cut eight pairs of rectangles.

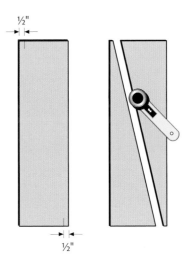

½"

½"

//

2 Sew each print triangle to a white triangle to make two small left-diamond units. Press the seam allowances toward the print triangle. Make 16.

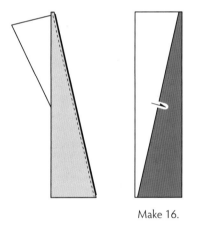

Make 16.

3 Trim each small left-diamond unit to measure 4½" x 16½". First, measure 4½" from the white edge and trim the excess from the print edge. Then trim the top of the unit so that the point of the print triangle is ⅛" wide, making the cut perpendicular to the side edges. Finally, measure 16½" from the top edge and trim the excess from the bottom of the rectangle.

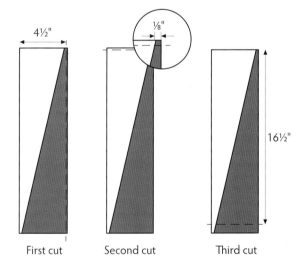

4 Place a black-and-white rectangle on a white 5¼" x 18" rectangle with right sides together. Measure and mark ½" from the top-right and bottom-left corners. Cut the stacked rectangles in half from mark to mark as shown. Repeat to cut eight pairs of rectangles.

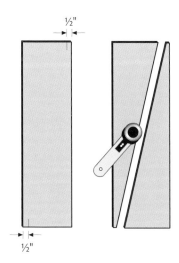

5 Sew each print triangle to a white triangle to make two small right-diamond units. Press the seam allowances toward the print triangle. Make 16.

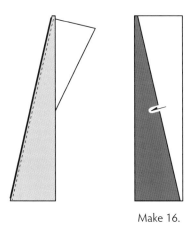

Make 16.

6 Repeat step 3 to trim each of the small right-diamond units.

Making the Large Units

Stitch all pieces with right sides together using a ¼" seam allowance.

1 Stack one red rectangle and one white 9¼" x 18" rectangle with right sides together. Repeat steps 1 and 2 of "Making the Small Units" to make two large left-diamond units.

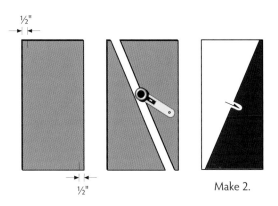

Make 2.

2 Trim each large left-diamond unit to measure 8½" x 16½". First measure 8½" from the white edge and trim the excess from the red edge. Trim the top of the unit so that the point of the red triangle is ⅛" wide, making the cut perpendicular to the side edges. Finally, measure 16½" from the top edge and trim the excess from the bottom of the rectangle.

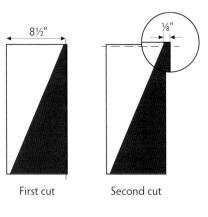

First cut   Second cut

Third cut

3 Place the remaining red rectangle right sides together with a white 9¼" x 18" rectangle. Repeat steps 4 and 5 of "Making the Small Units" to make two large right-diamond units.

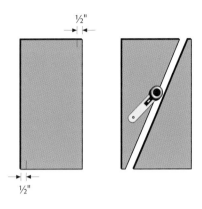

Make 2.

4 Repeat step 2 to trim each of the large right-diamond units.

Assembling the Bed Runner

1 Lay out the small- and large-diamond units as shown, creating two rows of 18 units as shown below.

2 Sew the units together in rows. Press the seam allowances to the left in the top row and to the right in the bottom row.

3 Join the rows to complete the runner top. Press the seam allowances in one direction.

Finishing the Bed Runner

For more information on any of the following steps, download free illustrated instructions at ShopMartingale.com/HowtoQuilt.

1 Cut the backing fabric to measure 38" x 86". Layer and baste the backing, batting, and bed-runner top.

2 Quilt as desired. The sample is quilted with diagonal lines that echo the pieced diamonds.

3 Trim the backing and batting even with the runner top.

4 Using the black-and-red print strips, bind the edges of the bed runner.

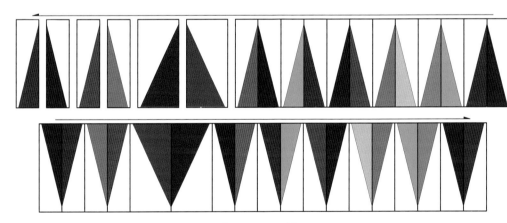

Runner assembly

Fireworks

By using the same cream fabric in both the pieced and alternating blocks, Doug created a runner of stars that explode from the background like fireworks in the sky.

By Doug Leko

FINISHED SIZE: 31" x 83"

Materials

Yardage is based on 42"-wide fabric. The bed runner shown was made using the Old Glory Gatherings fabric collection by Primitive Gatherings for Moda Fabrics.

1¾ yards of cream tone on tone for blocks

1⅓ yards of dark-blue print #1 for blocks, outer border, and binding

⅝ yard of dark-red print for blocks and inner border

⅜ yard of dark-blue print #2 for blocks

⅜ yard of light-blue print for blocks and middle border

⅓ yard of beige print for blocks

¼ yard of tan print for blocks

2⅝ yards of fabric for backing

37" x 89" piece of batting

Cutting

From dark-blue print #1, cut:

1 strip, 3½" x 42"; crosscut into 2 squares, 3½" x 3½". Trim the remainder of the strip to 2⅝" wide; crosscut into 8 squares, 2⅝" x 2⅝".

1 strip, 2½" x 42"; crosscut into 8 squares, 2½" x 2½". Trim the remainder of the strip to 2⅜" wide; crosscut into 8 squares, 2⅜" x 2⅜".

6 strips, 3½" x 42"

6 strips, 2½" x 42"

From the cream tone on tone, cut:

1 strip, 3½" x 42"; crosscut into 8 squares, 3½" x 3½"

1 strip, 5" x 42"; crosscut into 8 rectangles, 2" x 5". Trim the remainder of the strip to 4½" wide; crosscut into 4 squares, 4½" x 4½".

2 strips, 3½" x 42"; crosscut into 24 rectangles, 2" x 3½". Trim the remainder of the strip to 2⅜" wide; crosscut into 8 squares, 2⅜" x 2⅜".

2 strips, 2¾" x 42"; crosscut into 16 squares, 2¾" x 2¾". Cut the squares in half diagonally to make 32 triangles.

1 strip, 2⅝" x 42"; crosscut into 8 squares, 2⅝" x 2⅝"

1 strip, 2½" x 42"; crosscut into 12 squares, 2½" x 2½"

4 strips, 2" x 42"; crosscut into 72 squares, 2" x 2"

2 strips, 12½" x 42"; crosscut into 6 rectangles, 8½" x 12½"

From the tan print, cut:

1 strip, 3½" x 42"; crosscut into 16 rectangles, 2" x 3½"

From the beige print, cut:

1 strip, 3½" x 42"; crosscut into 8 squares, 3½" x 3½". Trim the remainder of the strip to 2½" wide; crosscut into 4 squares, 2½" x 2½".

2 strips, 2" x 42"; crosscut into 24 squares, 2" x 2"

From the dark-red print, cut:

1 strip, 3½" x 42"; crosscut into:
   16 rectangles, 2" x 3½"
   2 squares, 3½" x 3½"

1 strip, 2½" x 42"; crosscut into 8 squares, 2½" x 2½"

5 strips, 2" x 42"

Continued on page 55

Continued from page 53

From the light-blue print, cut:

1 strip, 2⅜" x 42"; crosscut into 8 squares,
    2⅜" x 2⅜". Trim the remainder of the strip to
    2" wide; crosscut into 8 squares, 2" x 2".
6 strips, 1¼" x 42"

From dark-blue print #2, cut:

2 squares, 4½" x 4½"
2 squares, 3½" x 3½"
2 strips, 2¾" x 42"; crosscut into 16 squares,
    2¾" x 2¾". Cut the squares in half diagonally to
    make 32 triangles.

COORDINATED EFFORT

Choose a tan print with a blue design
to coordinate with the other fabrics in
block A. Likewise, select a beige print
with red in its pattern to coordinate
with the colors in block B.

Making Block A

For all blocks, stitch all pieces with right sides
together using a ¼" seam allowance.

1 Draw a diagonal line on the wrong side of each
2⅜" dark-blue #1 square. Place a marked square

on one corner of a cream 3½" square with right sides
together. Sew on the drawn line. Trim ¼" outside the
seamline and press the corner open, pressing the
seam allowances toward the center, to make a
3½" x 3½" A1 unit. Make eight.

A1 unit.
Make 8.

2 Sew two cream triangles to opposite sides of a
2⅝" dark-blue #1 square. Sew two more cream
triangles to the remaining sides of the dark-blue
square to make a 3½" x 3½" A2 unit. Make eight.

A2 unit.
Make 8.

3 Place a cream 2" x 3½" rectangle on one end
of a tan 2" x 3½" rectangle, right sides together,
with the rectangles lying perpendicular to each other.
Draw a line from corner to corner as shown on page
56 and sew along the line. Trim ¼" outside the
seamline and press the seam allowances toward
the cream fabric.

4 Draw a diagonal line from corner to corner on the wrong side of a cream 2" square. Place the square on the opposite end of the tan rectangle and sew on the drawn line. Trim ¼" outside the seamline and press the seam allowances toward the cream triangle to make a 2" x 5" A3 unit. Make eight.

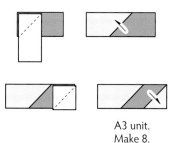

A3 unit.
Make 8.

5 Draw a diagonal line from corner to corner on the wrong sides of two cream 2" squares. Place a marked square on one end of a tan 2" x 3½" rectangle. Sew on the drawn line. Trim ¼" outside the seamline and press the seam allowances toward the corner.

6 Place the second marked square on the opposite end of the tan rectangle and sew on the drawn line. Trim ¼" outside the seamline and press the seam allowances toward the corner to complete a 2" x 3½" A4 unit. Make eight.

A4 unit.
Make 8.

7 Draw a diagonal line from corner to corner on the wrong side of each 2½" dark-blue #1 square. Place two marked squares on diagonally opposite corners of a cream 4½" square as shown, right sides together. Sew ¼" from both sides of the drawn line. Cut on the drawn line and press the seam allowances toward the dark triangles.

8 Place a marked square on the remaining corner of each unit as shown. Sew ¼" from both sides of the drawn line. Cut on the drawn line and press the seam allowances toward the dark triangles to make four A5 units. Trim, if necessary, to measure 2" x 3½". Make eight A5 units.

A5 unit.
Make 8.

9 Sew an A4 unit to the bottom of an A1 unit and press the seam allowances toward the A4 unit. Stitch an A3 unit to the right edge of the assembly and press the seam allowances toward the A3 unit to make a corner square. Make eight.

Corner square.
Make 8.

10 Sew an A5 unit to the bottom of an A2 unit to make a side unit. Press the seam allowances toward the A5 unit. Make eight.

Side unit.
Make 8.

11 Arrange four corner squares, four side units, and one 3½" dark-blue #1 square as shown. Sew the units together to assemble block A, pressing the seam allowances as indicated by the arrows. Trim and square up the block to measure 12½" x 12½". Make two.

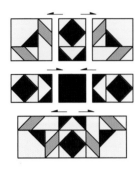

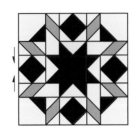

Block A.
Make 2.

Making Block B

1 Draw a diagonal line from corner to corner on the wrong sides of 16 cream and 16 beige 2" squares.

2 Place a marked beige square on the left end of a dark-red 2" x 3½" rectangle as shown. Sew on the drawn line. Trim ¼" outside the seamline and press the seam allowances toward the corner. Repeat to add a cream square to the right end of the dark-red rectangle, creating a 2" x 3½" B1 unit. Make eight.

B1 unit.
Make 8.

3 Repeat step 2, changing the directions of the seamlines to create a B2 unit. Make eight.

B2 unit.
Make 8.

4 Draw a diagonal line from corner to corner on the wrong side of a cream 2½" square. Place a marked square on a beige 2½" square and sew ¼" from both sides of the drawn line. Cut on the drawn line and press the seam allowances toward the cream triangles to make two half-square-triangle B3 units, each 2" x 2". Make eight.

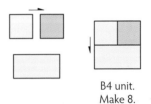

B3 unit.
Make 8.

5 Sew a cream 2" square to the left side of a beige 2" square as shown to make a two-patch unit. Stitch the two-patch unit to the top of a cream 2" x 3½" rectangle to make a 3½" x 3½" B4 unit. Make eight.

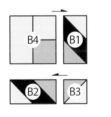

B4 unit.
Make 8.

6 Arrange one each of units B1–B4 as shown and sew together, pressing the seam allowances as indicated by the arrows, to make a 5" x 5" corner square. Make eight.

Corner square.
Make 8.

7 Draw a diagonal line on the wrong side of 16 cream 2" squares. Place a marked square on one corner of a beige 3½" square as shown on page 58. Sew on the drawn line. Trim ¼" outside the seamline and press the seam allowances toward the corner.

8 Place a second marked square on an adjacent corner of the beige square as shown. Sew, trim, and press as before to complete a 3½" x 3½" B5 unit. Make eight.

B5 unit.
Make 8.

9 Draw a diagonal line from corner to corner on the wrong side of each dark-red 2½" square. Follow steps 7 and 8 of "Making Block A" on page 56 to make eight B6 units, using the dark-red squares in place of the dark-blue squares.

B6 unit
Make 8.

10 Sew a B6 unit to the bottom of a B5 unit as shown to make a side unit. Press the seam allowances toward the B6 unit. Make eight.

Side unit.
Make 8.

11 Arrange four corner squares, four side units, and one dark-red 3½" square to make block B. Sew the units together and press the seam allowances as indicated by the arrows. Square up the block to measure 12½" x 12½". Make two.

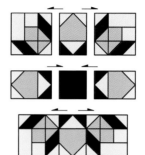 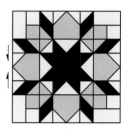

Block B.
Make 2.

Making Block C

1 Draw a diagonal line from corner to corner on the wrong side of each cream 2⅜" square. Place a marked square on a light-blue 2⅜" square with right sides together and sew ¼" from both sides of the drawn line. Cut on the drawn line and press the seam allowances toward the cream triangle to make two C1 units measuring 2" x 2". Make 16.

C1 unit.
Make 16.

2 Arrange two C1 units, a light-blue 2" square, and a cream 2" square as shown. Sew the pieces together in rows and press the seam allowances in alternating directions. Join the rows and press the seam allowances in one direction to make a 3½" x 3½" C2 unit. Make eight.

C2 unit.
Make 8.

3 Sew a cream 2" x 3½" rectangle to the left side of a C2 unit. Press the seam allowances toward the rectangle. Stitch a cream 2" x 5" rectangle to the top of the unit to make a corner square. Press the seam allowances toward the rectangle. Make eight.

 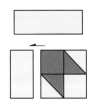

Corner square.
Make 8.

4 Sew two dark-blue #2 triangles to opposite sides of a cream 2⅝" square. Sew two more dark-blue #2 triangles to the remaining sides of the cream square to make a 3½" x 3½" C3 unit. Make eight.

C3 unit.
Make 8.

5 Draw a diagonal line from corner to corner on the wrong sides of the remaining eight cream 2½" squares. Follow steps 7–8 of "Making Block A" to make eight C4 units, substituting the cream squares for the dark-blue squares and 4½" dark-blue #2 squares for the large cream squares.

C4 unit.
Make 8.

6 Sew a C4 unit to the bottom of a C3 unit as shown to make a 3½" x 5" side unit. Press the seam allowances toward the C4 unit. Make eight.

Side unit.
Make 8.

7 Arrange four corner squares, four side units, and one 3½" dark-blue #2 square as shown. Sew the pieces together to make block C, pressing the seam allowances as indicated by the arrows. Square up the block to measure 12½" x 12½". Make two.

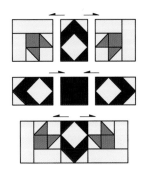 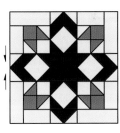

Block C.
Make 2.

Assembling the Bed Runner

1 Arrange the A, B, and C blocks and cream 8½" x 12½" rectangles as shown in the assembly diagram on page 60. Sew a cream rectangle to each pieced block to create a row. Press the seam allowances toward the cream rectangles.

2 Join the rows to complete the runner center. Press the seam allowances in one direction.

3 Sew the short ends of the dark-red 2" x 42" strips together to make a long strip. Crosscut the strip into two 72½" lengths and two 23½" lengths.

4 Sew the 72½" strips to the long edges of the runner. Press the seam allowances toward the border. Stitch the 23½" strips to the short ends of the runner and press the seam allowances toward the border.

5 Sew the short ends of the light-blue 1¼" x 42" strips together to make a long strip. Crosscut the long strip into two 75½" lengths and two 25" lengths. Sew the strips to the runner as in step 4. Press the seam allowances toward the middle border.

6 Sew the short ends of the 3½" x 42" dark-blue #1 strips together to make a long strip. Crosscut the strip into two 77" lengths and two 31" lengths. Sew the strips to the runner as in step 4. Press the seam allowances toward the outer border.

Finishing the Bed Runner

For more information on any of the following steps, download free illustrated instructions at ShopMartingale.com/HowtoQuilt.

1 Cut the backing fabric to measure 37" x 89". Layer and baste the backing, batting, and bed-runner top.

2 Quilt as desired. The sample is quilted with winding feathers and flames in the center and rows of circles, spirals, and more feathers in the borders.

3 Trim the backing and batting even with the runner top.

4 Using the 2½"-wide dark-blue #1 strips, bind the edges of the bed runner.

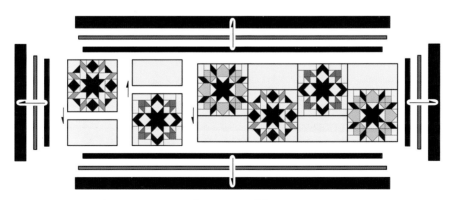

Runner assembly

Linked

Subtle prints link rectangular blocks into a soothing and restful whole, while the hue and value contrast keep the woven chains clearly visible.

By Stephanie Prescott

FINISHED SIZE: 25½" x 80½"

Materials

Yardage is based on 42"-wide fabric. Fat quarters are approximately 18" x 21". The bed runner shown was made using the Kahuna Batiks and Hot Off the Press fabric collections by Stephanie Prescott for Fresh Water Designs with E.E. Schenck Company.

1 fat quarter *each* of 5 assorted blue prints
    for blocks

1 fat quarter *each* of 5 assorted gold prints
    for blocks

½ yard of gold print for binding

2½ yards of fabric for backing

31" x 86" piece of batting

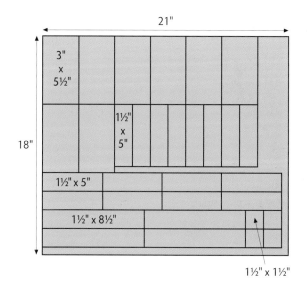

Cutting

Refer to the cutting guides at right for making the best use of your fabrics.

From *each* of the assorted blue prints, cut:
8 rectangles, 3" x 5½" (40 total)
16 rectangles, 1½" x 5" (80 total)
4 rectangles, 1½" x 8½" (20 total)
4 squares, 1½" x 1½" (20 total)

From *each* of the assorted gold prints, cut:
8 rectangles, 1½" x 10½" (40 total)
8 rectangles, 2½" x 5½" (40 total)
8 rectangles, 1½" x 2½" (40 total)
16 squares, 1½" x 1½" (80 total)

From the gold print for binding, cut:
6 strips, 2½" x 42"

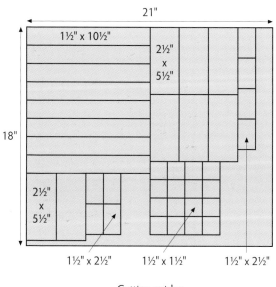

Cutting guides

Preparation

1 Sort the blue and gold pieces into 20 piles for block A, each containing one 1½" x 1½" square and two 3" x 5½" rectangles of the same blue print, plus two 1½" x 2½" and two 2½" x 5½" rectangles of the same gold print.

2 Sort the remaining blue and gold pieces into 20 piles for block B, each containing one 1½" x 8½" rectangle and four 1½" x 5" rectangles of the same blue print, plus two 1½" x 10½" rectangles and four 1½" x 1½" squares of the same gold print. Work with one pile at a time as you make the blocks.

Making Block A

Stitch all pieces with right sides together using a ¼" seam allowance.

1 Sew a blue 1½" square between two gold 1½" x 2½" rectangles to make a three-patch strip. Press the seam allowances toward the gold rectangles.

2 Stitch gold 2½" x 5½" rectangles to the sides of the three-patch strip. Press the seam allowances toward the gold rectangles.

3 Sew blue 3" x 5½" rectangles to the sides of the unit to complete block A. Press the seam allowances toward the blue rectangles and trim the block to measure 5½" x 10½". Make 20.

Block A.
Make 20.

Making Block B

Stitch all pieces with right sides together using a ¼" seam allowance.

1 Sew a blue 1½" x 8½" rectangle between two gold 1½" squares to make a three-patch strip. Press the seam allowances toward the gold squares.

2 Stitch gold 1½" x 10½" rectangles to the top and bottom of the three-patch strip. Press the seam allowances toward the gold rectangles.

Assembling the Bed Runner

1 Lay out the A and B blocks in an alternating arrangement, as shown below.

2 Sew the blocks together in rows. Press the seam allowances toward the A blocks.

3 Join the rows to complete the runner top. Press the seam allowances in one direction.

Finishing the Bed Runner

For more information on any of the following steps, download free illustrated instructions at ShopMartingale.com/HowtoQuilt.

1 Cut the backing fabric to measure 31" x 86". Layer and baste the backing, batting, and bed-runner top.

2 Quilt as desired. The sample is quilted with simple lines (straight and curvy) that emphasize the pieced shapes.

3 Trim the backing and batting even with the runner top.

4 Using the gold 2½"-wide strips, bind the edges of the bed runner.

3 Sew a gold 1½" square between two blue 1½" x 5" rectangles; make two. Press the seam allowances toward the gold square. Sew three-patch strips to the top and bottom of the unit from step 2 to complete block B. Press the seam allowances toward the center unit and trim the block to measure 5½" x 10½". Make 20.

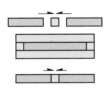

Block B.
Make 20.

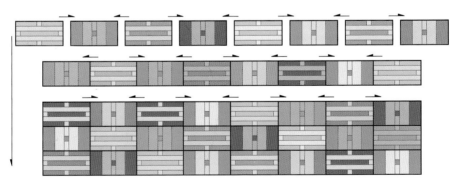

Runner assembly

Bold and Bright

Wild Goose Chase

Flying Geese are quite versatile because they can look modern or traditional, depending on the use and placement of fabrics, and you can use many or just a few. Here, the bright colors on a neutral background make this bed runner a standout.

Designed and pieced by Audrie Bidwell, and quilted by Laura McCarrick

FINISHED SIZE: 30½" x 99½"

Materials

Yardage is based on 42"-wide fabric. Fat quarters are approximately 18" x 21" and fat eighths are approximately 9" x 21". The bed runner shown was made using various fabrics by Tula Pink for FreeSpirit Fabrics and the Classic Essentials fabric collection by P&B Textiles.

2⅞ yards of light-gray solid for blocks and background

1 fat quarter of teal tone on tone for blocks

1 fat eighth *each* of green, pink, orange, coral, raspberry, lime, aqua, and yellow tone on tone for blocks

⅛ yard of black solid for blocks

⅝ yard of fabric for binding

3 yards of fabric for backing

36" x 105" piece of batting

UNBOUND BY CONVENTION

If you prefer a scrappy binding, like that of the sample bed runner, use 2½"-wide strips of assorted fabrics instead of a single color. One strip, 2½" x 42", *each* of seven fabrics is enough to bind the runner.

Cutting

From the light-gray solid, cut:
6 strips, 3⅜" x 42"; crosscut into 68 squares, 3⅜" x 3⅜"*
13 strips, 5½" x 42"; crosscut 7 of the strips into:
    1 rectangle, 5½" x 14½"
    1 rectangle, 5½" x 15½"
    1 rectangle, 5½" x 24½"
    1 rectangle, 5½" x 25½"
    1 rectangle, 5½" x 29½"
    1 rectangle, 5½" x 30½"
    1 rectangle, 5½" x 34½"
    1 rectangle, 5½" x 35½"

From the black solid, cut:
8 squares, 3⅜" x 3⅜"

From *each* of the green, pink, orange, coral, raspberry, lime, and aqua tone on tones, cut:
2 squares, 6¼" x 6¼" (14 total)

From the yellow tone on tone, cut:
3 squares, 6¼" x 6¼"

From the teal tone on tone, cut:
4 squares, 6¼" x 6¼"

From the fabric for binding, cut:
7 strips, 2½" x 42"

*If your fabric is narrow, you may need to cut an additional strip.

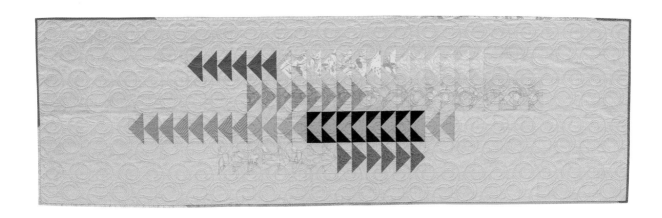

Making the Flying-Geese Units

Stitch all pieces with right sides together using a ¼" seam allowance.

For speedy results, this project uses the four-at-a-time method to make the flying-geese units. The 6½" squares will form the larger triangles and the 3⅜" squares will form the smaller side triangles.

1 Draw a diagonal line from corner to corner on the wrong sides of the eight black and 68 light-gray 3⅜" squares.

2 Place two marked light-gray squares on opposite corners of a green 6¼" square as shown. Sew ¼" from both sides of the drawn line. Cut on the drawn line to make two partial units. Press the seam allowances toward the small triangles.

3 Place another light-gray square on the remaining corner of each partial unit as shown. Sew ¼" from both sides of the drawn line. Cut on the drawn lines to make four flying-geese units. Press the seam allowances toward the small triangles. Trim, if needed, to measure 3" x 5½".

4 Repeat steps 2 and 3 to make a total of eight light-gray/green flying-geese units.

Make 8 total.

WORKING IN MULTIPLES

Each set of one large and four small squares will make four flying-geese units. The pattern calls for flying geese to be made in sets of 6, 8, or 12. Where only six are needed, make one set as instructed and then discard one partial unit at step 3. Alternatively, make all eight flying-geese units and use the extras for a pillow top or to add to the back of your bed runner. You will need to cut additional 3⅜" squares to make the extra units.

5 Repeat steps 2 and 3 as necessary to make a total of 76 flying-geese units as shown, substituting black 3⅜" squares for the light-gray squares in eight of the teal flying-geese units. You'll need six each of the aqua, pink, teal, and raspberry/light-gray units; eight each of lime, coral, orange, and green/light-gray units; eight teal/black units; and 12 yellow/light-gray units.

Make 6 of each. Make 8 of each. Make 12.

Assembling the Bed Runner

1 Arrange the flying-geese units by color in four rows as shown. Sew the flying-geese units together in each row. Press the seam allowances toward the bases of the large triangles.

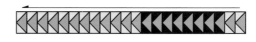

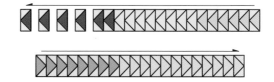

2 Stitch the light-gray 5½"-wide rectangles to the ends of the flying-geese rows as shown in the assembly diagram below. Press the seam allowances toward the light-gray strips.

Adding the Border

1 Sew three light-gray 5½" x 42" strips together end to end to make a long strip. Trim the long strip to 5½" x 99½". Make two.

2 Sew a strip to each long edge of the runner center as shown in the adding-borders diagram below. Press the seam allowances toward the light-gray strips.

Finishing the Bed Runner

For more information on any of the following steps, download free illustrated instructions at ShopMartingale.com/HowtoQuilt.

1 Cut the backing fabric to measure 36" x 105". Layer and baste the backing, batting, and bed-runner top.

2 Quilt as desired. The sample is quilted with an overall design of swirls.

3 Trim the backing and batting even with the runner top.

4 Using the 2½"-wide strips of fabric for binding, bind the edges of the bed runner.

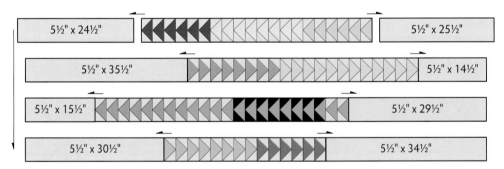

Runner assembly

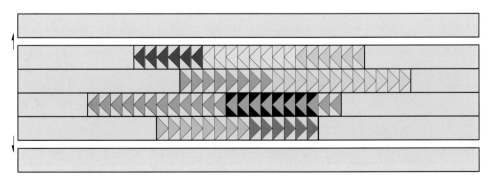

Adding borders

Jewel Rings

Based on an English-paper-piecing project called the Ferris Wheel, this bed runner is a lovely pattern of rings made from squares, 60° triangles, and hexagons. Yes, it involves Y-seams, but there's really no cause for concern—the instructions will take you through the process step by step.

Designed and pieced by Audrie Bidwell, and quilted by Laura McCarrick

FINISHED SIZE: 29½" x 95½"

Materials

Yardage is based on 42"-wide fabric. Fat quarters are approximately 18" x 21". The bed runner shown was made using Sketch (in black) by Timeless Treasures Fabrics and assorted solids by Kona Cottons for Robert Kaufman Fabrics.

2⅜ yards of black tone on tone for blocks, border, and binding

1 fat quarter *each* of 12 assorted solid colors for blocks

2⅞ yards of fabric for backing

35" x 101" piece of batting

Template plastic

Preparation

Trace one copy each of patterns A–D (pages 76–78) onto template plastic. Cut out the pieces to use as templates. You may prefer to create full patterns for A and C from folded paper before making the templates.

VERY VARIED

The yardage requirements provide enough fabric to cut extra colored squares and triangles, allowing more choices when you make the runner top. You may find it helpful to lay out all the colored squares and triangles before you begin piecing, to ensure a good distribution of the colors throughout the runner. Any extra pieces can be used on the back of the bed runner or to make a coordinating throw pillow.

Cutting

From the assorted fat quarters, cut *a total of:*
26 squares, 6½" x 6½"
22 D triangles

From the black print, cut:
5 A hexagons
2 B triangles
2 B triangles, reversed
4 C triangles
6 strips, 4" x 42"
7 strips, 2½" x 42"

SEWING Y-SEAMS

Set-in seams, or Y-seams, are sewn where three or sometimes four pieces meet at a single corner intersection. The finished construction looks like the capital letter Y.

Begin and end sewing ¼" from the ends of each seamline, where indicated by dots on the patterns and in the illustrations, unless you're stitching all the way to the outer edge of the runner. This allows the seam allowances to separate as you set in the third piece of the Y-seam for more accurate and attractive seam intersections. You may find it useful to mark the seamline intersections on the wrong sides of the fabric pieces to indicate where to begin and end the seams.

- Pin the first two pieces to be joined with right sides together and stitch the seam, beginning and ending at the dots ¼" from the fabric edges and backstitching the seam ends to secure the stitches.

- Swing the first piece out of the way. Pin the third piece to the second piece and stitch, beginning at the dot or seam intersection.

- Fold the second piece out of the way and align the edges of the first and third pieces in the group. Pin and stitch, beginning at the central seamline intersection where the dot is.

Making the Full Blocks

For all blocks, stitch all pieces with right sides together using a ¼" seam allowance.

1 Sew a D triangle to a contrasting 6½" square, beginning and ending the seam ¼" from the fabric edges as shown and backstitching the seam ends to secure. It may be helpful to mark a dot ¼" from each corner to aid you when sewing. Press the seam allowances toward the square. Make 18 units.

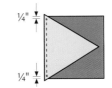

Start and stop ¼" from edge.

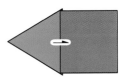

Make 18.

2 Using a Y-seam technique, stitch one triangle/square unit to an A hexagon as shown, starting and stopping ¼" from each end of the square. (That means you'll be sewing right up to the spot where the square has been joined to the triangle.) Press the seam allowances toward the hexagon.

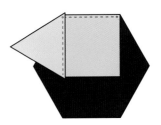

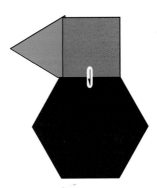

3 Sew the square of a second triangle/square unit to the triangle of the first triangle/square unit as shown. Press the seam allowances toward the square. Pivot the unit for the Y-seam technique and stitch the second square to the hexagon. Press the seam allowances toward the hexagon.

4 Repeat steps 2 and 3 to add a total of six triangle/square units to the hexagon, creating a full block. Make three.

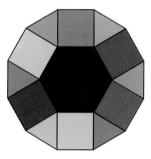

Make 3.

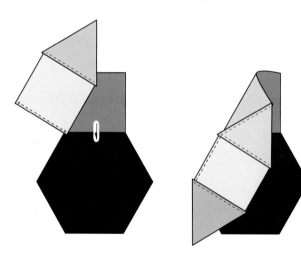

Making the Partial Blocks

1 Sew a D triangle between two contrasting 6½" squares as shown, using the Y-seam technique. Press the seam allowances toward the squares. Make four units.

Make 4.

2 Stitch one unit to an A hexagon as shown, starting and stopping ¼" from each end of the squares and breaking the seam at the triangle point. Press the seam allowances toward the hexagon.

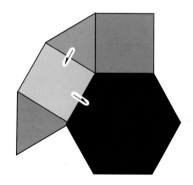

3 Sew a second unit to the opposite side of the hexagon to make a partial block. Make two.

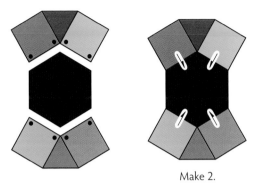

Make 2.

Assembling the Bed Runner

1 Arrange the full and partial blocks as shown in the adding-borders diagram at right, matching the seam intersections. Sew the blocks together with the Y-seam technique, breaking the seamlines at the triangle points.

2 Sew the B and B-reversed triangles to the ends of the runner as shown. You can stitch all the way to the fabric edge on the outer edges of the runner.

3 Use the Y-seam technique to stitch a C triangle to each inside corner along the sides of the quilt as shown. Trim the edges of the runner evenly, remembering to include ¼" for seam allowances.

4 Sew the black 4" x 42" strips together end to end to make a long border strip.

5 Measure the short dimension of the runner top and cut two strips from the border strip to that measurement. Sew one strip to each short end of the runner and press the seam allowances toward the strips.

6 Measure the long dimension of the runner top, including the borders, and cut two strips from the remainder of the border strip to that measurement. Sew one strip to each long edge of the runner and press the seam allowances toward the strips.

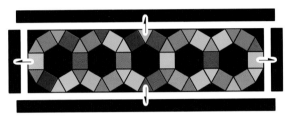

Adding borders

Finishing the Bed Runner

For more information on any of the following steps, download free illustrated instructions at ShopMartingale.com/HowtoQuilt.

1 Cut the backing fabric to measure 35" x 101". Layer and baste the backing, batting, and bed-runner top.

2 Quilt as desired. The sample is quilted with rows of a loop-de-loop design. Trim the backing and batting even with the runner top.

3 Using the black 2½"-wide strips, bind the edges of the bed runner.

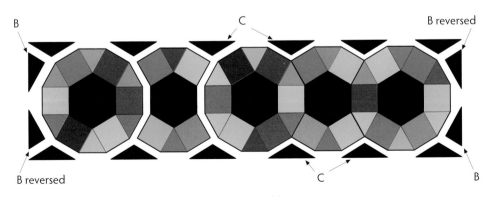

B   C   B reversed

B reversed   C   B

Runner assembly

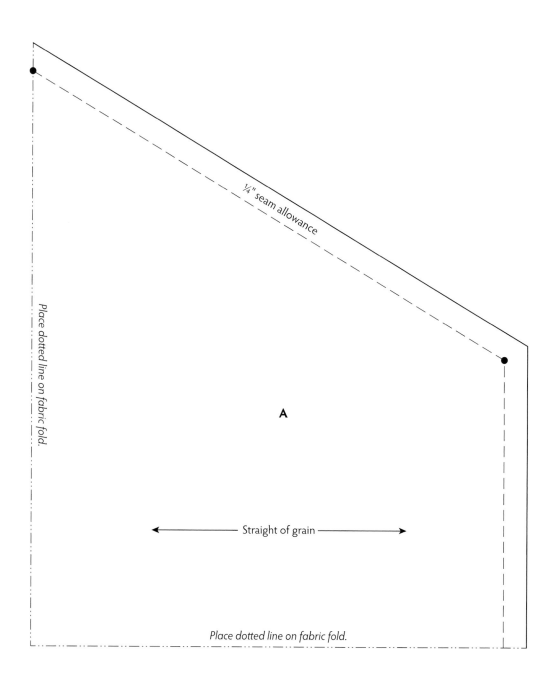

¼" seam allowance

A

Place dotted line on fabric fold.

Straight of grain

Place dotted line on fabric fold.

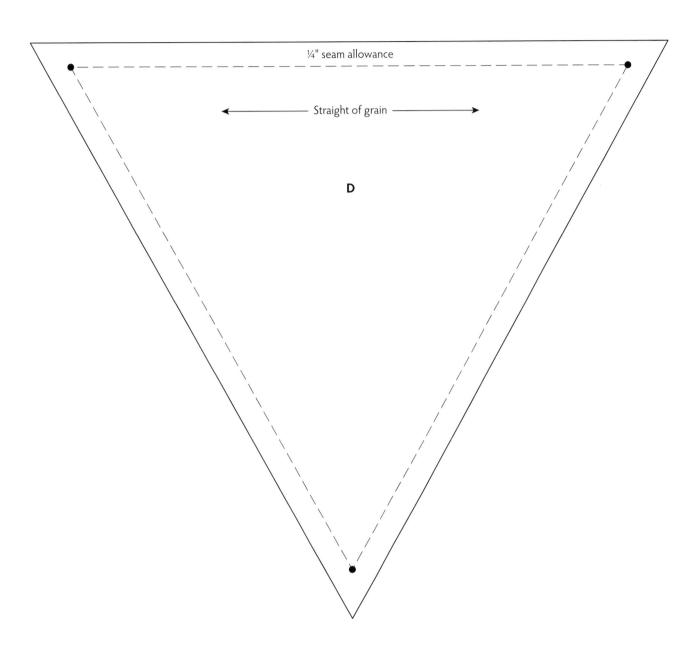

¼" seam allowance

Straight of grain

D

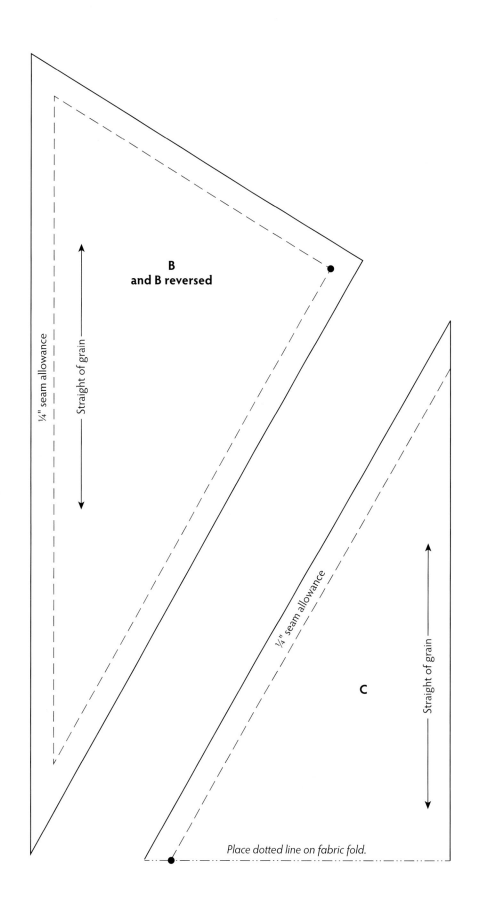

B
and B reversed

¼" seam allowance

Straight of grain

¼" seam allowance

Straight of grain

C

Place dotted line on fabric fold.

ABOUT THE CONTRIBUTORS

Heather Andrus and Megan Jimenez

Heather and Megan are sisters who blog and write patterns at Quilt Story. They've both sewed since they were teenagers and began quilting and writing patterns in 2007. Heather and Megan are busy stay-at-home moms with eight children between them. Along with quilting they love sewing pillows, bags, clothing for their babies, and home-decor items and gifts. Meet these sisters at Quilt-Story.com or on Instagram: @quiltstory and @quiltstorymeg.

Audrie Bidwell

Born in Singapore and raised in Australia, Audrie found quilting after she moved to the United States. Quilting was the perfect outlet for her creativity, and has led her to a community she is proud to be part of. Audrie loves working with bright colors and drawing inspiration from traditional designs. She lives in Connecticut with her husband and two Ragdoll kitties. You can find her online at BlueIsBleu.blogspot.com, where she chronicles her life and loves.

Brigitte Heitland

Brigitte's design background inspired her to create quilts that impress with their clear, peaceful, and refreshing look. The simple, minimalistic patterns surprise the viewer, and the generous use of solids enhanced by splashy bits of prints prove her beautiful sense of style, color, and design. Brigitte is a fabric and pattern designer. She designs for Moda and is the owner of Zen Chic. She has three children and lives with her family in Germany.

Kimberly Jolly

Kimberly is the owner of Fat Quarter Shop, an online fabric store, and It's Sew Emma, a pattern company. Kimberly has been quilting for more than 15 years. Her designs are often inspired by vintage quilts and blocks, but she occasionally ventures out to try something fresh and new. Kimberly loves to create quilts for friends and family, especially her children, who are a constant source of inspiration.

Amanda Leins

Amanda, a recovering classical archaeologist, uses timeless classical elements as a basis for her quilt designs. Incorporating proportion and balance, color and playfulness, with solid workmanship, she believes that the quilts we make today become a part of the historical record and go on to live their own lives and tell their own stories. A professional long-arm quilter, Craftsy instructor, book author, and pattern designer, Amanda has seen her work juried into an MQX (Machine Quilters Exposition) show. She lives in Saratoga Springs, NY, with her husband, two kids, and one crotchety old cat.

Doug Leko

Doug is a uniquely talented young quilt designer who founded Antler Quilt Design in 2008. His reputation has grown along with his business, and he now has a vibrant and growing collection of patterns available at quilt stores around the US and Canada, as well as online at AntlerQuiltDesign.com. His work has been featured in *McCall's Quilting, Quiltmaker,* and *American Patchwork & Quilting.*

Stephanie Prescott

Stephanie was a shop owner for 13 years before throwing herself into the pattern- and fabric-design arena full-time. Her goal in designing is to create something fun, interesting, and inspiring to make. She is passionate about mixing eclectic fabrics with contrasting patterns for added texture and movement. As a self-proclaimed math nerd, Stephanie is inspired by geometry in architecture, nature, and art. Her soul is endlessly inspired by her two children. See more of Stephanie's designs at AQuiltersDream.com.

Heidi Pridemore

Born and raised in Rochester, NY, Heidi received a bachelor's degree in industrial design from Rochester Institute of Technology. In 2000, she began working in the fabric industry, designing projects for numerous fabric companies. Today she also designs patterns and fabrics for her business, The Whimsical Workshop, as well as for magazines such as *Quiltmaker, McCall's Quick Quilts, The Quilter,* and *Quilt.* She has authored five quilting and craft books. When not designing and traveling to trade shows and lectures, she enjoys staying at home in Arizona with her husband and design partner, Matthew.

Jocelyn Ueng

Jocelyn is the design director for pattern company It's Sew Emma. She claims to be a novice quilter, but working in the quilting world for several years has changed the way she looks at all things. Jocelyn loves to extract designs from her surroundings and her biggest emphasis is on versatility of design. She wants others—no matter their taste—to be able to use her designs to create original pieces that will be loved.